ENCOURAGEMENT

ENCOURAGEMENT

REFRESHING OTHERS WITH
A WORD FITLY SPOKEN

JOHN LEHMAN

First Edition, Hardback: 2018

Printed in the United States of America

ISBN: 979-8-9864349-1-9

Published by www.greatwriting.org

Cover design by Greg Warner

Appreciations

Knowing the difficult days the disciples would encounter after His ascension, Jesus spent much time with those chosen few giving them words of encouragement (John 14-17). God has used John Lehman's long-standing pastoral ministry to similarly encourage those facing hard times. With this book John seeks to equip fellow-believers to imitate their Lord as they minister comfort and encouragement to one another and to the hurting world around them. Though the book is small, the need for encouragers is great in these latter days before the Lord returns.

Jim Berg, DMin

Professor of Biblical Counseling, BJU Seminary, Greenville, SC

Sadly, all around us there are downcast and discouraged people. But Pastor John Lehman has written an encouraging book, encouraging Christians to be encouragers of others! Having read the ten chapters, I can vouch for their being soundly biblical, sympathetically pastoral, eminently readable, exceedingly helpful, and realistically practical.

It was a privilege to have a preview of this timely book, and it is a privilege to commend it to the wider Christian community. Read and heed!

Encouragement is perhaps as neglected a ministry as it is a needed ministry. This book, however, will reveal that, by God's grace you, too, can be a Barnabas—a son (or daughter) of encouragement—putting courage, hope and confidence into others.

Timothy Cross, BA, BD, Th.D. Litt.D

Cardiff, Wales

This easy-to-read work on encouragement did what it was intended to do for me—encourage! At the same time, it provided me with insight, confidence, and additional biblical guidance so that I might more consistently encourage others. In an extremely comforting way, John walks the reader through a variety of principles and real-life opportunities to be an encourager; but what I like most is how effectively he threads God's Word throughout every chapter. If you are wondering: How can I be more positive, more uplifting, and more like Christ in my daily life? Consider a deep dive into this book for guidance from someone who walks the talk!

Brent Heidorn, Ph.D.

Associate Dean for Research and Assessment,

College of Education, University of West Georgia

The application of encouragement in the local body is the lynchpin of a healthy, vibrant church. It reflects the believer's desire to foster love and build spiritual enrichment in the lives of others; especially those facing spiritual oppression and trials on a daily basis. This book is invaluable to the life of the believer as it serves to guide in cultivating what may not come natural to us— the building of the local body and edification of the saints by the conveyance of kind words. I strongly encourage you to take these words and richly apply the concepts to those God has placed within your circles.

Jack Martin

Deacon and Co-Laborer, Hampton Park Baptist Church, Greenville, SC

I know of no one that has been more consistently encouraging to me than John Lehman! When it comes to encouraging others, we need to learn from him. I trust God will use this book to help us recover the lost art of encouraging others.

Jeremy McMorris

Lead Pastor, Liberty Baptist Church, Dalhart, TX

God's Word is clear: "Death and life are in the power of the tongue, and those who love it will eat its fruit" (Proverbs 18:21). As Christ's redeemed, our words can indeed be *lifegiving.* Such was the case with Jonathan's counsel to his friend David when he "encouraged him in God" (1 Samuel 23:16). *Encouragement* is likewise a gift to those who *need* and desire to *give* encouragement through words. In this excellent resource Dr. John Lehman uses the brushstrokes of wit, wisdom, hymns, history, and outstanding quotations to lead the reader into a deeper understanding of biblical encouragement. He carefully demonstrates that encouragers must find their traction in personal humility and concern. He also concludes each of the ten chapters with *Points for Awareness and Action* to help facilitate personal application, group discussion, and counseling home-work. And he tethers this entire topic to the gospel. This book is a gift to Christ's people!

Dr. Jim Newcomer

Senior Pastor, Calvary Baptist Church of Ypsilanti, MI; Adjunct Professor, Virginia Beach Theological Seminary & Bob Jones University/Seminary

This book wisely unpacks from scriptural instructions and examples what it means to speak words of encouragement and how to speak such words. The layout is very easy to follow. Practical exercises are included which will help the reader to apply what he has been learning. I am sure that you will be edified as you read it.

Jim Newheiser

Director of the Christian Counseling Program, Associate Professor of Practical Theology, Reformed Theological Seminary, Charlotte, NC

The words on these pages clearly reflect the heart of a faithful biblical counse-lor. They are carefully considered and well outlined. Dr. Lehman is a living example of the truths he expounds, giving greater authenticity to his message of encouragement. With his predictably gentle tone, the author inspires the encourager to be more intentional in his ministry to those who are anxious and downhearted in a troubled world. The principles outlined are not limited by cultural boundaries, making this a practical tool for all who serve in faraway places. This is a must-read for everyone with a heart to serve the Lord.

Dave Rudolph

Missionary Church Planter, South Africa

The book is great; I read it and it was a huge encouragement for me and my family. I was born in and am serving for the Lord in Pakistan. I lost my job, but this book gave me great encouragement. Pastor John Lehman gave lots of references and good ideas by the leading of the Holy Spirit for the hopeless people, for the broken hearts of people, and for those who don't trust in the Lord. The book is simple blessing for all hopeless people.

Pastor Shaukat Siddique

Bible Believers Baptist Church, Lahore, Pakistan

Encouraging others is such an inexpensive way to treat so many downcast people, change a day from gloomy to sunny, and to give just that little word that can make such a difference. And it can be done with sincerity and honesty. This book is so good; I will want to buy some copies for gifts.

Naomi Taylor

Retired Church Administrator, Greenville, SC

Purpose

It has been well said that "in the middle of every difficulty lies an opportunity." But not everybody who is experiencing a set of difficult circumstances feels that way.

This little book maps out some of the DNA of encouragement and draws several lines of illustration and application to show you how you can be an encourager of others in these needy days!

Over the years, many people have
encouraged me, and I have endeavored to do
the same to others as they navigate life's
challenging journey. I hope that you, too, will
find encouragement as you read these pages
and as you practice these principles in your
own life—as well as in the lives of others!

"A generous person will prosper;
whoever refreshes others will be refreshed."
Proverbs 11:25 (NIV)

John Lehman

www.wordsfitlyspoken.info

Acknowledgments

When I was near the completion of my book *Fit for the Master*, our office manager, Naomi Taylor, at Hampton Park Baptist Church, Greenville, SC, mentioned that I ought to think about writing a book on Encouragement. It took my mind back twenty-four years earlier. A few months after I arrived as a staff pastor in the fall of 1994, the first sermon I preached was from Proverbs 25:11. Shortly after that, I began teaching a counseling course to our laypeople which I entitled *Words Fitly Spoken*. That theme rang loudly with me. The topic has been one that has run through my mind, but through Naomi's *encouragement* I began pondering the culmination of the same.

Naomi has consistently and encouragingly helped me get started, and finalize, this book. Her *words fitly spoken*, whether in her office, at church, or in daily projects, have all added to my motivation to complete this task. I thank her for her faithful encouragement in my life . . . she's been a wonderful example of one who works tirelessly for the cause of Christ, and seeks to help others be their best. It's been my privilege to work alongside one who encouraged me by her own embodiment of loving God and loving others!

Next, I'd like to thank Greg Warner for again helping me capture the contents of the book in the fine design and cover of the book. I know a book isn't to be judged by its cover, but I sure didn't want one to detract. If anything, Greg has helped me display the book contents in such a powerful way that I just hope the inside will live up to the outside!

I thank Jim Holmes for again "getting this book out of me"! (That's an inside joke, as one of the first comments he made to me before the writing of my first book was when he showed me a cartoon of a book being noticed by an X-ray radiologist—the book itself in the abdomen of a patient. The doctor's words to the patient were something like, "Hmm, I see there's a book in you; we're going to have to get that out of you!") He has not only been a publisher and editor, but also an encouraging friend as he has sought to direct and correct my content, as well as refresh my soul by praying for me and this project as the work continued to take shape and near completion.

I thank my wife, Suzie, for again encouraging me with this goal completion. As a self-published author, I, and we, have to store our inventory, and right now, every bed in our home has books beneath the mattresses and bed frames! She has helped me fix my eyes on the goal rather than allow them to get way-laid in the work or process. Whether I was excited about a portion of the book, or discouraged about another, she has kept me even-keeled to keep working toward the prize of another completed book.

Finally, I thank the Lord for giving me the idea to begin, and the strength to finish this work! Truly, the desire accomplished is sweet to the soul (Prov. 13:19) and I'm forever thankful that He has set desires and intents as a goal, and helped me work through to its completion. Many times, I have had the thought "I can do all things through Him who strengthens me!" It's a blessing to have such a wonderful resource of Jesus to rely upon during the easier times as well as the more difficult ones!

Dedication

I praise the Lord for gifting me with a mom who embodied the word "Encourager"! She was one who loved to praise the Lord and lift up others. She didn't look to be encouraged, but sought to do that to everyone around her. Throughout her life, she wanted no attention brought upon or about her, but always sought to bring that to others. She was the consummate hostess, most suitable help meet to my dad, and the best mom a young son—or older son—could want!

God, in His infinite wisdom and timing, called her to enter heaven's gates when she was just sixty-six years old. I don't know of anyone who knew her, whether as a lifelong friend or one who had recently become acquainted with her, that didn't say something to the effect that she had been an encouragement to them.

In memory of her, and her devotion to encourage, I dedicate this book to F. Nadine Dodds Lehman!

Chapter Contents

Purpose 9

Acknowledgments 11

Dedication 13

Preface 16

1 Encouragement in Society
(In Common Thinking Today) 21

2 Encouragement in Scripture
(In Spiritual Understanding) 26

3 Encouragement in Speech
(In Words Fitly Spoken) 34

4 Encouragement in Example
(In Living and Modeling Intentionally) 48

5 Encouragement in the Past
(In the Expression of Others) 59

6 Encouragement in Kindness
(In Showing Tender Care) 68

7 Encouragement in Lifestyle
(In Natural Day-to-Day Living) 74

8 Encouragement in Priorities
(Putting First Things First) 83

9 Encouragement in Friendship
(In the Care and Nurture of Others) 92

10 Encouragement in Consecration
(In Living Life Wholly for God) 99

Appendix 1: Quotable Quotes to Think About 103

Appendix 2: Bible Texts to Think About 105

Books that Helped Me 107

Resources 108

Connect with John Lehman 109

John's Other Books 110

Preface

The emphasis in this book is on how you might be an encouragement to others. It is a wonderful emphasis, and one that Scripture supports completely. But at the same time, it takes great resources in your own soul to be able to encourage others, especially when you are undergoing difficulties in your own life.

God, through David's own life, demonstrates how people may continue to be encouraged in their own souls, which then enables them to encourage others, even when they themselves are going through significant struggles and difficulties. There is an interesting passage in 1 Samuel 30 to illustrate this.

With his military background and experience, David was quite the warrior, and so much so that God even had to refrain from allowing him to build the temple, no matter how much he, David, wanted to. As a result of his kingly leadership, he was at the forefront of many battles. And, he also had many loyal and devoted men who were not only soldiers with him, but his personal friends. One day, his character and leadership were put to the test when he and his men returned to their city after being away on military duty.

When they returned to Ziklag, the Amalekites (David's enemies) had conducted a raid against the city, and had taken captive the women and all who were there at the time. They hadn't killed anyone, but they had taken them away.

When David and his men returned to the city and found it burned with fire, and that their wives and children were gone, they all mourned together. But, no sooner had they started to mourn over this situation, all of the warriors began to discuss stoning David, their leader.

At this point, David was himself quite upset that his family had been captured! He was sorrowful that they were gone, and certainly he didn't know if they were hurt or perhaps had even been killed. Not only did he personally experience this grief, but then he heard that the men were intending to stone him! They thought David was responsible for their families being taken captive, and they wanted to end his life.

WHAT A GREAT TESTIMONY AS TO WHERE

ONE MAY RECEIVE STRENGTH AND

SUSTENANCE—WHERE BETTER A PLACE TO

RECEIVE IT THAN FROM THE LORD!

Where was David to turn when all of life was crashing down upon him? Where could he go for encouragement? 1 Samuel 30:6 states that he "encouraged himself in the LORD his God" (KJV) or as it says in other Bible translations, "strengthened himself in the LORD." What a great testimony as to where one may receive strength and sustenance—where better a place to receive it than from the Lord!

So, after David was encouraged, he was then able to rally his troops to head back to find their wives and children. Between the men wanting to stone David, and his encouragement in the Lord, he was able to turn their sentiment to follow him again! The entire scene would have been so different had

David himself not turned the emotional tide by first being encouraged, and then helping his men to be encouraged. And, we know the end of the story now, but they didn't then. Yet, they still pursued, and conquered, receiving their families back. And, as Scripture stated, all was returned and nothing was lost!

Encouragers can find strength and encouragement from the Lord, and don't need anyone else to help them be encouraged! However, it is only fair to say that it takes a real and intense pursuit of God during these times of personal discouragement. So often, God uses other people—friends, family members, work colleagues, and other associates—in the process of encouragement. And we certainly need and benefit from it!

God is a very present help in times of trouble, so the word is this: be sure to go to Him for that help!

In the pages that follow, we will consider various facets of encouragement—what it is, why it is needed, how it may be given, and many more aspects of this wonderful quality!

GOD IS A VERY PRESENT HELP IN TIMES OF
TROUBLE, SO THE WORD IS THIS: BE SURE TO
GO TO HIM FOR THAT HELP!

Points for Awareness and Action

- David, a man after God's own heart, needed to be encouraged in sudden and unforeseen circumstances. He was intentional in finding his encouragement from the Lord.

- Suggest two or three ways in which you would identify and gently introduce encouragement to someone who is within your circle of influence. How would you need to prepare your heart for this first?

1

ENCOURAGEMENT
in
SOCIETY

In Common Thinking Today

May the God of endurance and encouragement grant you to live in such harmony with one another, in accord with Christ Jesus.

(Romans 15:5)

What Do People Say about Encouragement?

Encouragement, although people receive it and use it (and often even without thinking about it), is not something that has a vast amount of information either on its benefits or how to provide it. Encouragement, however, is one of the most popular ways that people express support for one another.

In 1956, Alfred Adler was one of the earlier psychologists to propose some theories about encouragement. He considered it a core feature of human development. He believed that human beings are specifically oriented toward social interest, which is a desire to belong and contribute to others and society. If and when people lose social interest, whether through discouragement or failure, they need encouragement, especially in regard to interacting with others.

It's for Everyone!

Encouragement is something romantic partners enjoy, athletic coaches use, parenting processes, leadership provides, and family involvement fosters. As we will see later, there is a vast range of Scriptures that relate to the need for encouragement. Although limited in how deeply they can provide detailed insights, studies have shown why encouragement is an important phenomenon to every individual.

It is considered that there are two parts of encouragement and the first is defined this way: "to provide encouragement is to inspire or help others, particularly toward a conviction that can work on defined solutions and that they can cope with any predicament."

Another way to consider encouragement is for it to be a non-verbal attitude that communicates a sense of esteem and worth to an individual. Two well-known authors, Nielly and Dinkmeyer, used this definition in 1971:

> Encouragement is the process of facilitating the development of a person's inner resources and courage toward positive movement.[1]

There are many forms of encouragement skills, including reflective listening, use of humor, communicating faith in others, smiling, nonverbal acceptance of others, expressing genuineness, pointing out others' strengths, and the positive reframing and validating of others' goals.

THE GOAL OF ENCOURAGEMENT IS NOT
SIMPLY TO CHANGE SOMEONE'S BEHAVIOR
BUT TO INSTILL IN OTHERS THE COURAGE
AND THE CONFIDENCE TO CHANGE.

The goal of encouragement is not simply to change someone's behavior but to instill in others the courage and the confidence to change. The goal of encouragement is, therefore, not to modify any behavior, but to modify the individual's motivation!

A second means of encouragement focuses on the core

---

[1] *The Psychology of Encouragement.* Further information on page 107 of this book.

features of a fully functioning person. The functions are as follows:

- a positive view of oneself;
- a positive view of others;
- being open to experiences, and
- a sense of belonging to others.

A major source of all this is having a positive view of oneself, a sense of belonging, and the courage to be imperfect.

With this short introductory chapter complete, and since all truth really is God's truth, we will now turn our attention to the Bible, the Word of God, to see what it has to say, and to see how it confirms the art of encouragement.

Points for Awareness and Action

- Suggest two examples of encouragement you have received in the past. One should be where there was the use of words in the encouragement you received, and the other should be an example of indirect or nonverbal encouragement. Which did you prefer? Why?

- Consider the four bullet points just before the end of the chapter you have read. Which of these four elements do you think you most need to concentrate on if you are to be an encouragement to other people?

2

ENCOURAGEMENT
in
SCRIPTURE

In Spiritual Understanding

Let no corrupting talk come out of your mouths, but only such as is good for building up, as fits the occasion, that it may give grace to those who hear.

(Ephesians 4:29)

A High Calling

As Christians, we've been given a high calling. We are set apart as faithful servants of Christ, to be transformed by the renewing of our minds, and to be agents of change and restoration in our broken world by being the salt and light of the earth. We have been created new, and we are image bearers of Christ to the world through our love for one another. What a high calling—and, quite frankly—what an intimidating calling!

Proverbs 16:24 helps us realize how important words can be: "Gracious words are like a honeycomb, sweetness to the soul and health to the body." We have the ever-present power to speak truth and life into the experiences of people. Speaking words of encouragement and affirmation that the Holy Spirit places on our hearts is a life-changing practice and very often it comes about as we demonstrate our obedience and humility. The term *encouragement* has the meaning of "to fill with courage or strength of purpose."

> WE ARE TO BE TRANSFORMED BY THE RENEWING OF OUR MINDS, AND TO BE AGENTS OF CHANGE AND RESTORATION IN OUR BROKEN WORLD BY BEING THE SALT AND LIGHT OF THE EARTH.

Words of affirmation call those in our lives to be better men and women. We can use our words to bring others down and point out their flaws, or we can look for qualities to find praiseworthy, and inspire them to further cultivate those aspects of the fruit of the Spirit in their lives.

We have seen the case for encouragement; we instinctively know how important it is and what happens when there is a lack of it. Everyone needs it, and yet not everyone receives it! No matter what any resource states, and whether we think people need it or not, the Bible has much to say about being an instrument of encouragement. If the Bible says that we should be an encouragement, and yet we are not an encouragement, we are guilty of going against a holy command!

Consider what Paul wrote in Ephesians 4:29: "Let no corrupting talk come out of your mouths, but only such as is good for building up, as fits the occasion, that it may give grace to those who hear."

> WE INSTINCTIVELY KNOW HOW IMPORTANT ENCOURAGEMENT IS AND WHAT HAPPENS WHEN THERE IS A LACK OF IT. EVERYONE NEEDS IT, AND YET NOT EVERYONE RECEIVES IT!

Taking this verse at face value, one initially realizes that this New Testament proverb speaks loudly to a very important truth: we are to encourage! Paul writes, first of all, that we are never to have any disapproving or discouraging comment come out of our mouth. How easy is it to be negative? How easy is it to be discouraging? VERY! Because we are selfish beings, we look at circumstances only from our own perspective, and if we are not satisfied with them, we may find that we are really disparaging in the way we respond to others and to our circumstances.

God knew what He was doing when He told people that they should love their neighbor as themselves! We love ourselves. Face it, we do. We would rarely admit that, but it is indisputable that we love ourselves very much. People try hashtags to stress putting others first, and how our priorities should be for the advancement of others, and that is a sincere desire. But, truth be known, God determined that the best litmus test for us to use in measuring our love for others would be for us to make note of how much we love ourselves. As a consequence (and as a measuring stick), we are to love "our neighbors" to the same degree that we love and care for ourselves, just as Jesus said in giving the greatest commandment:

You shall love the Lord your God with all your heart and with all your soul and with all your mind. This is the great and first commandment. And a second is like it: You shall love your neighbor as yourself. On these two commandments depend all the Law and the Prophets. (Matthew 22:37-40)

The next point that the apostle Paul makes is that to keep us from corrupting speech, we should always seek to build others up and be positive; in other words, he is saying, "Be an encourager!"

In James chapter 3, we are told that

> . . . every beast and bird . . . can be tamed by mankind, but no human being can tame the tongue. It is a restless evil, full of deadly poison. With it we bless our Lord and Father, and with it we curse people who are made in the likeness of God. From the same mouth come blessing and cursing . . . these things ought not to be so. Does a spring pour forth the same opening both fresh and salt water?

The point is that good words and bad words should not come out of the same mouth. If we are to keep ourselves from discouraging talk, then we must use encouraging words. We ought not to do both.

> THE POINT IS THAT GOOD WORDS AND BAD WORDS SHOULD NOT COME OUT OF THE SAME MOUTH!

The letter to the Ephesians was written in such a way that it clearly leaves its mark among other Bible books by displaying the powerful impact of the gospel of Christ Jesus, whether on the life of an individual or on the corporate life of believers. Ephesians chapters 1-3 thoroughly expound the gospel while chapters 4-6 provide a very clear picture of how those doctrines change our lives. You might often hear the saying, "Live out the gospel of Jesus Christ." As you use this verse, along with the many others in these chapters, it will enhance that testimonial display of being a Christian, a "little Christ," to the world!

Ephesus was a large, prosperous harbor city. One of the Seven Wonders of the World was right there in Ephesus; it was the huge temple dedicated to a goddess named Diana. The sin the city promoted, and the wickedness of the known world at the time, made living like Christ an even greater challenge for believers there, and the contrast between their lives and the lives of others in the city was noteworthy. Light is the brightest when it is set against the darkest backdrop. In this case, because there was such sinful and lewd living, it was, without doubt, easy for believers to become discouraged and to live in the same way as others, and especially in light of the values the city promoted. However, here God says, through Paul, that His people are not to live like the earthly city or place where they live, but rather to live in character with the Heavenly City to which they are destined.

> LIGHT IS THE BRIGHTEST WHEN IT IS SET
> AGAINST THE DARKEST BACKDROP.

God specifically emphasizes to us, in His word, that we are to be mindful of what we say. And not only are we to be mindful of what we say, but we should use our words in such a way as to be a help or encouragement to others, giving some form of motivation to them that they would want to be better after what we've said to them than they were before.

There are numerous Bible texts on encouragement and examples of encouragement in action. To read these in some detail, please consult Appendix 2.

Points for Awareness and Action

- Think about the words of Paul in Ephesians 4:29: "Let no corrupting talk come out of your mouths, but only such as is good for building up, as fits the occasion, that it may give grace to those who hear." What are you going to do in order to encourage people who hear the words you speak?

- God has given us His Word, a word not only to teach, rebuke, and correct, but also to train us in righteousness. Do you love His Word, the Bible? Identify one other verse in this chapter that will inspire you to encourage others. Then think of how you could apply the principles to help a friend or family member.

3

ENCOURAGEMENT
in
SPEECH

Words That Are Fitly Spoken

And let us consider how to stir up one another to love and good works, not neglecting to meet together, as is the habit of some, but encouraging one another, and all the more as you see the Day drawing near.

(Hebrews 10:24-25)

A Case Study

Proverbs 25:11 provides the backdrop for a word that has been fitly spoken. Think about what took place when Solomon received this particular gift. Here was the king who had everything—wisdom, wealth, fame, just to mention a few—so when he received the gift that he mentions in this verse, it seems that it had such an effect on him that he penned the words: "A word fitly spoken is like apples of gold in a setting of silver."

Solomon himself probably spoke 3,000 proverbs, as it is recorded in 1 Kings 4:32. He probably wrote the book of Proverbs as a letter to his own sons. A proverb is used specifically to develop a wise, skillful approach to living.

So what Solomon was doing here was emphasizing what a proverb really was. A proverb has three characteristics: the first is *few words*, the second is *right sense*, and the third is a *fine image*.

Think about this particular proverb. A word that is fitly spoken is like apples of gold in settings of silver. That is really a very few words in which to say so much! The words that are spoken can be used in such a way to impact a person's life! Basically, in an even shorter format, words are gifts!

Think about gifts that you may have received in the past, or heard about from others. People are familiar with so-called white elephant gifts. They are called gifts because they are veiled behind wrapping paper or placed in a gift box but typically they are more of a joke and are meant for a person to have fun with than they are really intended to fulfill a person's desire.

Most people are familiar with someone who gives a sweater that is the wrong size, the wrong color, and the wrong name brand, and yet still considers that a gift. More than likely the person who receives that gift is going to leave it in the closet until the next opportunity to regift it to someone else! A true gift (using the sweater as the example) would be one that is the right color, the right size, and even has the right name brand; that will really be a gift that will be worn and used!

SOLOMON'S GIFT HAD SUCH AN EFFECT ON HIM THAT HE PENNED THE WORDS: "A WORD FITLY SPOKEN IS LIKE APPLES OF GOLD IN A SETTING OF SILVER."

A proverb also has *right sense*. Think about what point is being made in this verse. It is simply Solomon's desire, in this case, not only to help his sons, but all the others that read what he said, to think about the way they speak. It is so easy to verbalize, but at times to be unthinking and unkind in what you state. Solomon is specifically making the point that to really be worthwhile in your conversation, you should be sure that the words you use will be of the character that is mentioned here — that they will be fitly spoken. There needs to be proper thought put into what is said rather than the mere verbalization of them, whether to just be heard or to make one's point.

In the third aspect of this proverb there is a *fine image*. To put it another way, Solomon is giving all of us an opportunity to visualize what a word that is fitly spoken can really be equated to. As mentioned, this proverb may well have come about as a result of a gift that had been given to Solomon. Think about a man who had everything. He not only asked God for wisdom, but God wonderfully granted him riches. So for him to be king, to have wealth above all else, and, in addition, to have been given a gift and thus to make this response, is truly amazing. This gift may have been an item that had the appearance of a basket woven around gold balls, and was probably so striking in its appearance that Solomon exclaimed something like this: "Words that are spoken appropriately are special, and so like this gift here."

Being "The Greatest Ever"

Let me tell you something that happened when I was a boy. I can recall a rather embarrassing moment in my life, but, as time has gone by, it has made me realize why I spoke the way I did. Because my parents were missionaries in the Far East (our family lived in Taiwan), beginning in my first-grade year, I went to boarding school. I would see my parents at least once a month. As a parent (and now as a grandparent), I can hardly imagine sending off one of my children to be gone for up to three or four weeks at a time without seeing the child. In the early 1960s, there was no such thing as Skype. Moreover, there was very little phone usage even available on the island of Taiwan. So initially I did not have a whole lot of parental words to influence my life. I did have great dormitory parents and wonderful friends, but from the point of view of my relationship with my parents, there was great influence but there was not a lot of time I could spend with them.

While we were on deputation during my sixth-grade year, having just spent five years in boarding school, I was passing the time in the back seat of our car and I was doodling on some notepaper while we drove across state. Journeying on deputation was an enjoyable experience, but it also allowed for a lot of hours of boredom to set in because it involved traveling from city to city, and from state to state, for my dad to preach and present our ministry in various churches.

> I CONCLUDED MY DOODLING BY SIGNING
> OFF WITH MY NAME, INSCRIBING NEXT TO IT
> "THE GREATEST EVER."

The embarrassing moment I'm referring to came about like this: while I was writing something as the car sped along, I concluded my doodling by signing off with my name, inscribing next to it these words: "The Greatest Ever." I did not do this in a boastful or improper way, but my dad and mom both laughed at the fact that I described myself as "The Greatest Ever." Of course as all good parents would, they used the moment well to share with me that nothing and nobody was great except God, and I was definitely not God!

I am glad to say that I received the correction and clearly understood what they were saying. However as time passed, I came to a better understanding of why I had described myself as "The Greatest Ever." Somehow, in the few short days each month that they impacted my life during those times I was at boarding school, my parents made me feel as if I really was the greatest. They were not ones to spoil me or to let me have my way, but their words of affirmation and the recognition and display of their love and affection for me went well beyond the time they actually spent with me. Without me even knowing it, they had built me up in a truthful kind way as a parent would do, and made me feel I was loved and cared for far beyond anybody else. And I don't think that's such a bad thing for parents to make their children feel so affirmed that they might one day think that they're the greatest ever!

What the Term "Words Fitly Spoken" Really Means

Thinking about fitly spoken words, let's evaluate each one of these words. A "word" means counsel, instruction, encouragement, repute, reproof. So, considering the specific word that is being used, you need to be sure that it is one that is going to be moving in the right direction—and that it ends with inspiration on the part of the person who receives it. A word that is used in instruction must still carry with it empowerment and direction. A word used for encouragement must be thought of in such a way as to impact this life in a manner that it would never be directed without the influence of the person giving the encouragement. And at the same time, when there is reproof or correction, it should still be couched in such a way that it is received (or can be perceived) as a true and well-meant gift. Something that is said needs to impact the hearers in such a way that they will be the better because of what they heard. The word they were speaking about is not just a flowery compliment that is no more than fluff and proves to be without substance. And, it needs to be that which definitely encourages learning for life change, empowerment or correction.

IT MAY TAKE A LOT OF PRACTICAL

OBSERVATION FOR YOU TO BE SURE TO

EXPRESS WORDS APPROPRIATELY, TAKING IN

ALL THAT AFFECTS PEOPLE THROUGHOUT

THEIR DAY AND IN THE LIVES OF THEIR

NEIGHBORS AROUND THEM.

When you consider the phrase "fitly spoken," you think of the importance of being well suited to the occasion, well suited to one's character, or being well timed, well spirited, and well expressed. It may take a lot of practical observation for you to be sure to express words appropriately, taking in all that affects people throughout their day and in the lives of their neighbors around them. You need to be reminded of what is taking place when the conversation occurs, as well as taking into account how the other person will respond due to his or her very nature. What is discussed needs to be stated at the right time so that the other person is not too tired or when there is too much going on in the immediate environment. A great attitude needs to be there when the words are presented. And, kindness needs to surround how it is stated. Truth should always be spoken in love, and since one is never to lie, love must be used every time we speak!

So when one thinks of words being fitly spoken, there are some specific ways for this to take place.

TRUTH SHOULD ALWAYS BE SPOKEN IN

LOVE, AND SINCE ONE IS NEVER TO LIE,

LOVE MUST BE USED EVERY TIME WE SPEAK!

Characteristics of Fitly Spoken Words

The first is for it to be *well timed*. When words are presented, one needs to take into consideration everything that is happening at the time those words are pronounced. Not only today, but I am sure that throughout the time of the Bible being written, there were morning people and evening people. There were probably people who were very different in their mood before eating and after eating.

People live in a context of time and they either have busyness surrounding them—perhaps a swirl of noise and activity—or they may be facing a busy schedule with thoughts of upcoming activities surrounding and bombarding their minds. A word that is spoken in a fit and well-timed manner will make a tremendous difference. Sometimes, in circumstances such as those, it may be best not to even speak what you think is important; maybe it could be saved for a better, more appropriate, time.

A second way to make sure words are fitly spoken is to be sure they are *well suited to the occasion*. The occasion may be one where there is nervousness or anxiety or apprehension in the atmosphere. Or perhaps the person concerned is himself nervous and apprehensive. That man may have a lot of other things on his mind or that woman may be in a setting where she is not prepared to discuss (or even think about) a certain matter. You need to be sensitive and evaluate the whole occasion, and be sure that what you are thinking of saying to the individual concerned is going to help at that moment rather than to introduce a sense of unease or awkwardness.

YOU NEED TO EVALUATE THE WHOLE OCCASION, AND BE SURE THAT WHAT YOU ARE THINKING OF SAYING IS GOING TO HELP AT THAT MOMENT RATHER THAN TO INTRODUCE A SENSE OF UNEASE OR AWKWARDNESS.

Another aspect of using words fitly spoken is that they should be *well expressed*. The expressions that we make, or the kinds of body language we use, make a big difference in how words are received. Consider how gifts are given; think about a jewelry store and how a diamond is put on display. There is a beautiful background, perhaps a velvet one, that brings out the sparkle and beauty of that precious stone. That's how our expressions enhance what we say.

One of the most important things you wear is your expression! Think about what is said when it comes with a frown, a scowl or a smile. That's why God's Word tells us to speak the truth in love. God is not saying that we should candy-coat what we say—surely truth must be expressed. But, as Solomon has stated, what we say must be well expressed. A tone of voice that is harsh or critical can turn listeners away completely from being prepared to discuss a matter, whereas speaking to individuals in a tender and gracious tone is much more likely to bring about a response where they listen considerately and then take steps to change.

> A TONE OF VOICE THAT IS HARSH OR
> CRITICAL CAN TURN LISTENERS AWAY
> COMPLETELY FROM BEING PREPARED TO
> DISCUSS A MATTER.

Think about this statement: "That was great." If such a statement was uttered with no expression on the face and in a monotonous voice, the person hearing those words may well think the speaker was being sarcastic, critical or demeaning. However if the person said, "That was great!" and said it in an excited way with a pleasant smile and eagerness in her eyes, it would go a long way to reassuring the listener that what he or she had just done really was great!

For something to be fitly spoken also requires that it is *well spirited*. The attitude on display during the interaction makes all the difference in what is being said to the other person—and this applies whether encouraging or disciplining the person—and ensures that the outcome is still a gift in light of how fitly spoken these words have been!

WE ARE TO LOVE OTHERS IN THE SAME WAY
WE LOVE OURSELVES.
(MATTHEW 22:39)

Having the attitude of Christ, which is to esteem others better than oneself, should always be at the forefront of our minds when we are speaking! Christ says in the New Testament that we are to love others in the same way we love ourselves (Matthew 22:39). It is an amazing statement that Christ Himself recognizes and knows how self-centered we are and how much self-love we all have! Although elsewhere (in Philippians 2:3) He says through the apostle Paul that we are to esteem others better than ourselves (meaning that you should have the attitude of rising above the love you have for yourself and that you love others even more), He recognizes that we do, in fact, love ourselves; and if we could just see in what ways we love ourselves and recognize that—and then love others that much—we would always be well spirited in how we speak.

Finally, it needs to be *well suited to the character*. We not only need to consider what we say and how we say it, but to whom we are addressing our words. The matter of being well suited to the character means that it is important for us to take into account the temperament of the person we are speaking to. We need to be aware of how that person is going to react and respond.

When animal trainers consider obtaining and directing the animals they are to train, they study the temperament and the means and ways that the animal may respond to them. They learn so much about that animal before they begin the process of training it, and, by doing so, they know what will bring the most out of it as opposed to just mindlessly doing the same thing for every animal they come in contact with. If trainers such as these take that much time to consider something that does not even have a soul, how much more important is it for us, when we think of others and their circumstances (and as we keep in mind that they have souls and will live forever), to be thoughtful in how we speak to them.

As we continue the Proverbs 25:11 thought of apples of gold in settings of silver, the mental image is of golden fruit set in baskets which were, perhaps, chiseled vessels of openwork silver. The gift was original to the culture and was a silver woven style exterior with golden apples inside, almost looking as if there was a mesh netting, or basket, in its design. It involved an intricate silver sculpture with golden apples to be seen within the design. This inspired Solomon to make this strong visual comparison and so we today, likewise, may find it appealing.

Appropriate and properly timed words, whether a compliment or a rebuke, can be attractive and valuable, very much like the sight of gold apples set against the silver sculpture or carving, not unlike the way a picture frame enhances the picture.

Of course the Lord knows that it is easy to do all this to people who are good and kind, but it is really difficult to do this to those who aren't. God says in His Word that if we are kind to those who are kind to us, there is no difference at all in what we do. The Bible passage, Luke 6:32-33, reminds us that being kind to those who are kind to us, and loving those who love us, is not a great thing at all. What is really great, however, is to be kind to those who are unkind to us, and love those who are unloving toward us. In this way, we reflect the likeness of the Savior who came from heaven to redeem us and reconcile us to Himself even when we were His enemies.

We should so desire to have our words be fitly spoken that it will not matter how well we know someone—whether a first-time guest or a longtime friend or associate—and whether that person is nice or mean—but that we will be encouraging!

Points for Awareness and Action

- Words that are fitly spoken really originate in God, the giver of every good and perfect gift. You, as an image-bearer of God, are able to reflect His character in your speech.

- Think for a moment about the way you speak, and the words you use. James says some very important things about our speech and how we use our tongues. Think of three areas in the way you use your tongue that might need attention.

4

ENCOURAGEMENT
in
EXAMPLE

Living and Modeling Intentionally

Therefore encourage one another and build one another up, just as you are doing.

(1 Thessalonians 5:11)

Cultivating Godliness in Order to Be an Encourager

What does it mean to be godly? A godly person is one who ceases to be self-centered—and this is in order to become God-centered. Christ became a man and, as a result of His earthly ministry, we see how God intended for people to behave. Jesus is our unblemished example of godliness; therefore a godly person is a Christlike person.

Christianity with its goal of Christlikeness has a person in mind—and that person is Christ! What sets Christian spiritual victory apart from all other religions is that they have the knowledge of Christ as their goal—not moral perfection and not tranquility, although it is true that you will become more moral and your life will become more peaceful if you really are a believer. Because of the grace you have in Christ, the disciplines will do nothing to make you more accepted by the Father; you cannot be more accepted than you already are in Christ, since He has already done all the work involved in salvation for you.

To be like Christ won't just happen by going to church or thinking good thoughts or learning one Scripture or another; rather, it takes real discipline that will require focused thinking and living—the kind that Christ modeled during His brief life on earth.

How can it be in a world such as the one in which we live today (which requires us or entices us to pursue pointless gain) that we will achieve closeness with God? Part of the answer lies in the matter of how we acquire true discipline.

First, it is important to discipline yourself for an intimacy with God (1 Timothy 4:1-8). In this passage, verse 7 gives us the ultimate advice, and that is to discipline oneself for the purpose of godliness. In other words, Paul was saying to Timothy that he was to get serious about his walk with God because godliness does not just happen automatically or without effort.

Religion is not going to make it fair. We might find that we live in a kind of spiritual hothouse where people talk the talk but don't always walk the walk. In an artificial setting, it is so easy to act in a religious manner, and yet not to be truly godly. And in this way, it is possible for chilling religion slowly to cool the heart

THE PROBLEM THAT KEEPS US FROM BEING

GODLY IS A SPIRITUAL ONE.

So, my fellow believer, we must choose to discipline our lives so that they become more godly. The problem that keeps us from being godly is a spiritual one. Christians and non-Christians alike long for personal purity and power to live as their hearts tell them they should. But what we need is a deeper insight, practically speaking, into our relationship with God. In redemption we need an understanding that can guide us in constant instruction and interaction with the kingdom of God as a real part of our daily lives.

Cultivating the Right Kind of Lifestyle

For us to maintain godliness and discipline we must *first* of all make sure that our lives are very simple. Many of us face

50

similar obstacles. While some obstacles cause people to wallow in self-pity, others motivate folks to overcome great odds to be a success for God's glory! The desire to be intimate with God (and allowing that intimacy to grow into godliness) will cause you to become more focused in the things you do and therefore enable you to cultivate a simpler lifestyle.

> WHILE SOME OBSTACLES CAUSE PEOPLE TO WALLOW IN SELF-PITY, OTHERS MOTIVATE FOLKS TO OVERCOME GREAT ODDS TO BE A SUCCESS FOR GOD'S GLORY!

To begin this process, it may be necessary to make major changes. Most people today say yes to far too many things, and therefore end up with incredibly busy schedules. That means that they are busier than they need to be because they fear the void in their souls that a few quiet hours might otherwise reveal. If they are not careful, they will simply embrace busyness as a way of deadening the pain of an empty life. So to truly be disciplined, people really need to be more focused on what they say yes and no to.

Second, we must plan time for leisure and rejuvenation. Leisure and rejuvenation do not necessarily mean sitting still and meditating, but neither do they mean accomplishing the greatest athletic feat of your life. It requires people to consider what helps them to be more prepared to continue in their role or responsibilities, refreshed and prepared to keep on keeping on. Some people like quiet, so they need to be quiet; others love activity and accomplishment, so it is better for them to be mobile. Because there are responsibilities looming ahead, the best way to combat burnout is to have some change of pace built into one's life, and then following that time of rejuvenation, it will become apparent that more will be accomplished in the next segment than when there was no time set aside and one just kept hammering away at the project.

Third we must experience the joy of accomplishment. Solomon once said the desire accomplished is sweet to the soul, as is recorded in Proverbs 13:19. But with so much to do, we find that we have to be off to meet the next obligation and often we find that we never had the opportunity of savoring the job that was well done.

> TO BE TRULY DISCIPLINED, PEOPLE REALLY
> NEED TO BE MORE FOCUSED ON WHAT
> THEY SAY YES AND NO TO!

Fourth many people living in wealthier countries owe more than they can hope to repay, and debt has become a way of life for them. It is needful to remember that God said a good name is rather to be chosen than great riches (see Proverbs 22:1).

Fifth, most of us fool ourselves into thinking that with our modern technology we have simplified our lives. Truth be told, we have complicated them. Although technology is certainly a gift from God (He has allowed people to use their minds and skills to develop it), we must make sure that we use it to deepen our relationship with Christ rather than to distance it.

Balancing the Values and Principles

To maintain a simple life, it is important to make sure that there is time for God and that the lifestyle being adopted is suitably uncluttered. Consider Philippians 3:10—and the emphasis of the apostle, Paul, who makes it his main prayer that "I may know him," referring to the Lord Jesus Christ. Continuing in his writing, Paul states a few verses further on (vv. 11–14) that he "forgets those things that lie behind him and reaches forward to what lies ahead," meaning that he presses toward the goal for the prize of the upward call of God in Christ Jesus. In this sense, he first finds his encouragement in Christ, and, in this way, he will be able to infectiously pass it on to others!

The words of Proverbs 2:1-5 were given to Solomon to pass on to his son, and they were words of wisdom that could make us rich.

> My son, if you receive my words and treasure my commandments with you, making your ear attentive to wisdom and inclining your heart to understanding; if you call out for insight and raise your voice for understanding, if you seek it like silver and search for it as for hidden treasures, then you will understand the fear of the LORD and find the knowledge of God.

When one wants to be Christlike, 1 Corinthians 4:2 comes to mind. "Moreover, it is required of stewards that they be found faithful." For you to be faithful in the area of Christlikeness, and being one who encourages others, it is going to be vital that you keep showing up to do so. You do this by putting aside your own fears, uncertainties, and frustrations, and then focusing on the needs and situation of the other person. Consider Hebrews 12:1, a verse that makes the point to us that there is a great cloud of witnesses that are surrounding us. Because of that, we need to lay aside every weight or encumbrance, and sin must quickly be removed. Then we can run with endurance the race that is set before us. For folks to truly be able to encourage and motivate and inspire, they must make sure that the world's cares and temptations are not weighing them down.

And following verse 1, verse 2 makes the point that, for us to do this, we must fix our eyes on Jesus who is the author and perfecter of our faith, who for the joy that was set before Him actually endured the cross and despised—didn't worry about—the shame associated with it. Then, because of that, he was able to sit down at the right hand of the throne of God.

In Philippians 2:3-5, Paul gave four commands.

- We are to do nothing from selfishness or empty conceit;
- With humility of mind we are to regard others as more important than ourselves;
- We should not only look out for our own personal interests;

- Rather we are to look out also or instead for the interests of others.

God here speaks to us about having humility of mind and, as we have that humble mind, we will want to encourage others and empower them so that they will be more like Christ.

Surrender and Commitment

For you to sincerely desire to be like Christ, you must be willing to first of all surrender your *possessions* and your aspirations. It is vital that you declare God to be the owner of all. As you surrender all that you have to the One who enabled you to have it, you will find that you no longer just focus on yourself but realize that you are simply a steward. Therefore, you begin to seek to help others and build them up.

Your next step is to begin to surrender your *position* in life. You're not worried about what status you have attained. As you place everything you are before God in an act of commitment and dedication, you will find your security, your identity, and your peace in Him.

Third, surrender your *plans*. As the words of James 4:13-16 state, we must embrace the idea that it is only if the Lord wills it we will do this or that, whether in our business endeavors, our travel plans, or anything else in life.

Fourth, surrender your *people*—those who you love the most. You may be sure that God is in control. Realizing that what you do and what you say is to bring glory to God and good to others will motivate and challenge you to be an encourager as you want to uplift and edify them. Should God choose to allow one of your loved ones to pass away with some illness or difficulty, you've surrendered them to God anyway, so it will not stop you from doing what you need to do.

AS YOU SURRENDER ALL THAT YOU HAVE TO
THE ONE WHO ENABLED YOU TO HAVE IT,
YOU WILL FIND THAT YOU NO LONGER JUST
FOCUS ON YOURSELF BUT REALIZE THAT
YOU ARE SIMPLY A STEWARD.

In the fifth point, we must be people who *pray*. Prayer, simply explained, is communicating with God. This could be a conversation that is spoken aloud, silent in one's mind or heart, or even sometimes expressed in song. Many of the Psalms are prayers set to music. A primary purpose in prayer is to connect with God in order for Him to convey His will into our lives. It's actually cooperating with God to accomplish His goals in us and through us.

Effective prayer will have a believer specifically seeking the mind of God on a particular matter that's on his or her heart — whether it's confessing a sin, praising His name, pursuing His will, interceding for a friend or petitioning for our own needs, prayer must be God-centered and never self-centered. Sincere prayer comes from a heart that longs for God to reveal what He desires rather than what we want.

Prayer is not a *natural* response, but it is a *spiritual* one. If we are in tune with God and pursuing Him along with a life of godliness, we will desire to cultivate this discipline and we will do this often. Through the apostle Paul, God makes it clear that it is His will for us to pray without ceasing (1 Thessalonians 5:17). That doesn't mean we never do anything else, but it does mean we keep Him—God and His purposes for us—on our mind, in our heart, and in a pervading way; and as a result this will affect our attitude all the day long. God has revealed specifically, in Philippians 4:6, that we should be anxious for nothing, but that in everything by prayer and supplication with thanksgiving, we should let our requests be made known to Him.

There is an old song with the following words:

Why worry, when you can pray?
Trust Jesus, He'll be your stay.
Don't be a doubting Thomas,
rest fully on His promise,
Why worry, worry, worry, worry when you can pray?

I'm afraid that, today, we reverse that and say why pray when you can worry!

Points for Awareness and Action

- When we compare our lifestyles in our busy twenty-first century with the lifestyles of people in the New Testament, it is fair to say that we face particular challenges in how to keep in good spirits. (a) List the two greatest challenges to you and to others you know when it comes to overcoming discouragement. Then, (b), suggest how the Bible guides you to manage and overcome these challenges.

- The terms humility and Christlikeness have come up frequently in this chapter. Readers are encouraged to live a life of consecration to God. Think of two or three areas in your life that you might need to work on as you endeavor to develop or cultivate these graces. What strategies might you consider employing as you seek to live a life with clear and ongoing reference to God and His will in your day-to-day experience?

5

ENCOURAGEMENT
in
THE PAST

In the Expression of Others

Have I not commanded you? Be strong and courageous. Do not be frightened, and do not be dismayed, for the LORD your God is with you wherever you go.

(Joshua 1:9)

Developing Humility: What It Is to Be Humble

For us to be willing to encourage others, we must focus on becoming humble ourselves. Discipline is something that no one likes and yet which everyone admires! Discipline is something that great women and men exhibit behind closed doors, away from admiring fans and cheering crowds. Discipline is hard work done in obscurity for the sake of excellence. Disciplined people are almost always humble. They don't need cheering crowds to feed their hunger for excellence.

> HUMILITY IS A QUALITY OF ONE'S
> CHARACTER, AND NOT SOMETHING THAT A
> PERSON IS BORN WITH.

In the first place, to be humble does not mean it is simply an easy characteristic to model; rather, it is an intentional discipline. Humility is a quality of one's character, and not something that a person is born with.

Although humility is a Christlike virtue, it is frequently neither understood nor admired by most Western cultures. Most models of strong leadership consider it strange for someone to be thought of as humble.

Second, we may appreciate humility in others but we find that we rarely desire it for ourselves. The price is too high. Humility is not what gets us ahead, not on this earth, anyway, or so it seems. We want humble people around us because they are not a threat to us. Even Christ's disciples wanted to sit on either side of Him in positions that they considered would be places of prominence!

Third, humility is certainly not the result of having low self-esteem. There are some people who focus on their unworthiness or what they think are their wormlike qualities, justifying such a mindset by expressing the view that individuals amount to nothing apart from Christ. But that's not how Jesus came to us. To be truly humble, such a person must recognize everything he has is because he has received it from a loving Creator, and whatever he has received is to be used in a Christlike way in service to Him and the people He has created.

HUMILITY ISN'T THE RESULT OF HAVING A
POOR SELF-IMAGE, BUT COMES FROM A
PLACE OF STRENGTH AND INNER SECURITY.

So, while humility isn't the result of having a poor self-image, it does come from a place of strength and inner security. Genuinely humble people who have a desire to seek the well-being of others are generally very secure people. They are fully aware of their gifts, their training, their experience, and all the attributes that make them successful at whatever they do. That security, which is that honest healthy self assessment, results in more than a humble constitution, and it translates into actions that can be observed and actions that others will want to emulate.

Fourth, as a *discipline* we can measure our success in humility but as a *virtue* we cannot measure it. As soon as we think we are humble, in actual fact we are not! Genuinely humble people have a natural inattentiveness to it when it comes to the matter of their humility. They don't even think of themselves as humble. As a matter of fact they rarely think of themselves at all. Humble people are too occupied with the wellbeing of others to jealously guard their own interests or to notice their own self-importance.

For us to lift others up we have to be humble. If we exercise the discipline of humility long enough, it will inevitably permeate and dominate our nature without our knowing that it has happened. We will become oblivious to it.

To illustrate the point biblically, Mark 10:43-45 helps us to see the details. This is what Jesus said: "But whoever would be great among you must be your servant, and whoever would be first among you must be slave of all. For even the Son of Man came not to be served but to serve, and to give his life as a ransom for many."

The hymn written by Isaac Watts, *When I Survey the Wondrous Cross*, specifically clarifies this.

> When I survey the wondrous Cross,
> On which the Prince of glory died,
> My richest gain I count but loss,
> And pour contempt on all my pride.

Another important part of being an encourager is to have self-control. The flesh is most at home in the realm of wrong. I hardly need to say it again but we live in a world filled with twisted truth and distorted ethics. When you mix a flawed world with a failed nature, you've got the right combination for defeat. On the other hand, if you are a believer in Jesus Christ, you also have the Spirit of God living in you. According to Galatians 5:16, the only hope we have against slavish obedience to the flesh is the presence and help of the Holy Spirit. His recreating work in us gives us the opportunity to let Him have His way instead. In the words of the apostle Paul, "But I say, walk by the Spirit, and you will not carry out the desire of the flesh."

Galatians 5:19-21 records these words:

Now the works of the flesh are evident: sexual immorality, impurity, sensuality, idolatry, sorcery, enmity, strife, jealousy, fits of anger, rivalries, dissensions, divisions, envy, drunkenness, orgies, and things like these. I warn you, as I warned you before, that those who do such things will not inherit the kingdom of God.

But then note what the same apostle wrote in the verses following:

But the fruit of the Spirit is love, joy, peace, patience, kindness, goodness, faithfulness, gentleness, self-control; against such things there is no law. And those who belong to Christ Jesus have crucified the flesh with its passions and desires. If we live by the Spirit, let us also keep in step with the Spirit. Let us not become conceited, provoking one another, envying one another.

Sacrifice

Another matter of great importance is that of sacrifice. No other discipline is more closely associated with the character and the mission of Jesus Christ than sacrifice. Yes, He was intimate with God the Father, lived simply, sought solitude, surrendered his will to his Father daily, and lived a prayerful, humble life characterized by self-control. But it is sacrifice that distinguishes the Son of God from all figures in history and identifies Him as a Savior, even by those who scarcely know Him.

> IT IS SACRIFICE THAT DISTINGUISHES THE SON OF GOD FROM ALL FIGURES IN HISTORY AND IDENTIFIES HIM AS A SAVIOR.

What is sacrifice? What does becoming a sacrifice involve? To be sacrificial means that the ultimate hope in life is not to be self-centered but rather to be Christ-centered. Christ, through the apostle Paul, tells us to be a living sacrifice. Logically that does not make sense. Paul is asking us to put ourselves in a position that is cast down so that Christ can be lifted up. In Romans 12:1, Paul makes the point that our bodies and our lives should be a living sacrifice. This word *sacrifice* is only used a handful of times in all of his letters. He does not use it loosely. In Ephesians 5:1-2, Paul calls for us to be like Christ. In fact he states: "Therefore, be imitators of God, as beloved children; and walk in love, just as Christ also loved you and gave himself up for us, an offering and a sacrifice to God as a fragrant aroma."

As in all things, becoming a sacrifice requires a person to make a choice. To sacrifice is to give up something for the sake of something else that is much better. An offering is a voluntary act. Christ made that conscious choice to offer Himself as an atoning sacrifice so that He might have us as His own people. We are to make the same choice for the sake of knowing Him in a more intimate way—not to earn His pleasure or blessing, but as a means of coming to know Him more deeply.

> TO SACRIFICE IS TO GIVE UP SOMETHING
> FOR THE SAKE OF SOMETHING ELSE THAT IS
> MUCH BETTER.

For us to be sacrificial we must *first* of all understand that the devil hates it when people put God above all. He absolutely despises the Son of God, so the discipline that most reflects the Savior and his humility will be one that the devil will do his best to undo. The devil knows the power of the immediate and will try to convince you and me not to do what we should do.

Second, people will think you've lost your senses when you start to live a life of sacrifice. When you don't try to get more stuff or get ahead, they wonder why.

Third, you will panic because you think you are not getting far enough ahead or making progress at the speed you consider you should.

Fourth, your discipline will be tested repeatedly because the flesh seeks whatever will make it feel safe and comfortable.

Elizabeth Elliott's book *Through Gates of Splendor* introduces us to this event of sacrifice rather than human ease and gain. In it, she tells the wonderful story of lives lived well, lives lived for others, and in a way that is glorifying to God.

She personally recounts the spiritually stirring and physically gut-wrenching story of her husband, Jim, and his four missionary friends who wanted to spread the gospel to the Huaorani (Auca Indian) people of Ecuador. Full of joy and anticipation of what the gospel could do for these natives, unshackling them of their past sins and providing a hope for their future, they made several flights, providing a safe backdrop for when they landed and began to evangelize these dear folks who didn't yet know that Christ had died for them. For the sake of God's kingdom, these men finally believed it was time for them to land and personally encounter the Huaorani. Although it was believed that the Indians had somehow known these men didn't mean to do them evil, they still couldn't get over their past, and they massacred the missionaries in cold blood. What good came of this? We hear today the quote, "He is no fool who gives what he cannot keep to gain what he cannot lose." We will never know all of the reasons that these men lost their lives, but we do know one, and that is that they were willing to sacrifice their lives for the cause of Christ.

The application of this may be different for different people depending on their life circumstances, but it is necessary for us to live all out for the gospel, no matter where we are and no matter what we do. Sacrifice is no easy task, but it is certainly rewarding, for no one sacrificed more than God did in sending His Son, and that Jesus did in suffering through His death on the cross.

Points for Awareness and Action

- Humility is a wonderful grace; Jesus demonstrated it perfectly. In your daily walk with Jesus, and as you endeavor to become more and more like Him, suggest what your greatest priority should be as you live in a world that has wrong views of humility.

- Self control is listed as one aspect of the fruit of the Spirit. Read the whole list in Galatians 5:22-23 and make it a point of prayer that the Lord will help you cultivate the work of his Spirit in your life, especially in light of the natural impulses of the flesh that so often are in conflict with life in the Spirit.

6

ENCOURAGEMENT
in
KINDNESS

In Showing Tender Care

Let the favor of the LORD our God be upon us,
and establish the work of our hands upon us;
yes, establish the work of our hands!

(Psalm 90:17)

"Now faith is the assurance of things hoped for, the conviction of things not seen" (Hebrews 11:1). Chapter 11 of Hebrews is known by many as the "Faith Chapter." Reading through it, we see spiritual giant after spiritual giant being lauded by God for a willingness to follow God in fulfilling what He called them to do! And, you even note at the end of the chapter that "all these, though commended through their faith, did not receive what was promised..."

Faith is the reality that it is not *how well* we muster up our trust, but *in whom* we place our trust. As great as it is to read chapter 11 of Hebrews, these men and women were definitely being commended for the faith that they displayed. Reading through the list allows one to realize faith has been evident throughout God's historical dealings with mankind. Each hero of the faith lived and portrayed his or her belief in God by certain lifestyles and actions.

Faith requires us to believe with our mind while showing obedience with our body, all the while we never losing heart in the Object of our faith. There is relatively little need for emotion in faith. One doesn't feel faith; one lives faith.

Once people begin to live by faith, they start to display other characteristics, whether they feel the emotion or not. Kindness is a trait in one's life that many times is a reciprocal one. It's easy to be kind to those who are first kind to us, but God says for one to be kind when others are not is true Christlike kindness. Agape love occurs because of the need of the individual, not because of the individual's worth. Ephesians 4:32 makes it clear that for one to truly be Christlike, such a person must reveal kindness, tenderheartedness, and forgiveness. Nowhere in Scripture does it say a person is to act on feelings. There will be many times that feelings will try to redirect us from being kind, but knowing the object of our faith motivates us to be kind, no matter what.

What is kindness? Webster defines it as "the state, quality or habit of being kind; kind act or treatment; kind feeling; affection; goodwill." Synonyms of kindness or compassion are gentleness, benevolence, thoughtfulness, mercy, consideration, and helpfulness. Unkindness is defined as not sympathetic to or considerate of others; harsh, severe, cruel, rigorous, etc.

> SYNONYMS OF KINDNESS OR COMPASSION ARE GENTLENESS, BENEVOLENCE, THOUGHTFULNESS, MERCY, CONSIDERATION, AND HELPFULNESS.

We see that kindness consists in two parts: first, the feelings of compassion and motives of our hearts, and second, the resulting behavior that is intended for the improvement of another person's situation. Thus, kindness includes what is on the inside (and is therefore invisible to others) and what is exhibited (and is therefore visible to others).

Kindness manifests itself in words, actions, and nonverbal behavior; in essence, it is a broad dynamic. People exhibit kindness in varying degrees, from small, almost imperceptible acts, to life-encompassing acts. A truly kind person shows kindness habitually, in addition to performing purposeful acts of kindness. He or she shows concern and care for others and their needs and interests. A kind person does not play favorites but instead respects every individual as a created being. He or she is not sarcastic and will not take joy in the calamity of another. However, neither is the kind person wishy-washy. He is honest even when it causes pain, and he stands firmly on difficult principles, even when it is unpopular. The Christian loves the Lord above all, and God's law reflects God Himself. Therefore, kindness subjects itself to God's law, maintaining standards of right and wrong. The deepest motive of kindness stems from humility and gratitude to God for His wonderful gift of salvation.

A TRULY KIND PERSON SHOWS KINDNESS HABITUALLY, IN ADDITION TO PERFORMING PURPOSEFUL ACTS OF KINDNESS.

For one to truly be kind to those who are unkind requires a good measure of unselfishness. Sharing with others our words and finances reveals how unselfish we really are. A quote from Theodore Roosevelt brings this to mind: "No one cares how much you know until they know how much you care."

No one has it easy, and life doesn't always make sense. So, if everyone looks at his own difficulties, and considers how badly he has it, no one gets encouraged. Someone needs to break that cycle. God's Word in Philippians 4 tells us that "I can do all things through him [Christ] who strengthens me" and "I have learned in whatever situation I am to be content." So, with God, we can all do that is needed, and we can be content even if it doesn't end the way we want it to.

So, as Ephesians reminds us, "Let no corrupting talk come out of your mouth, but only such as is good for the building up, as fits the occasion, that it may give grace to those who hear!"

Kind Words

The point of Proverbs 25:11 is that a word fitly spoken is like apples of gold in settings of silver. Are our words really valuable like gold and silver? God's Word says they are. If that's the case, we have the ability to bestow great riches on others, no matter how poor we may be! What exciting opportunities await us!

So, please keep this in mind: good words honor and love God and my neighbor, they have a positive effect on others, they are true and kind, and they serve a good purpose. Good words have the power to heal individuals in relationships.

Writing under the inspiration of the Holy Spirit, the author of Hebrews reiterates this point in stating that "without faith, it is impossible to please him, for whoever would draw near to God must believe that he exists and that he rewards those who seek him" (Hebrews 11:6).

Points for Awareness and Action

- Kindness originates in God Himself. A discouraged person is very likely in need of expressions of kindness. Think of two or three ways in which you may show kindness to people you know.

- Read Ephesians 4:29, and, to begin with, consider how many times in a day you might be tempted to speak discouragingly. Then, try to change the cycle, and see whether you can speak encouragingly and give grace the same number of times the following day.

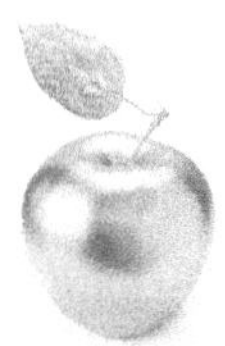

7

ENCOURAGEMENT
in
LIFESTYLE

Natural, Day-to-Day Living

But they who wait for the LORD
shall renew their strength;
they shall mount up with wings like eagles;
they shall run and not be weary;
they shall walk and not faint.

(Isaiah 40:31)

Uplifting Words

I read a story once about a boy who was so depressed that he decided to end his life by jumping off a bridge in New York City. He left a note saying that if anyone along the way would smile or speak a kind word to him, he would not go through with this plan. Nobody did, so he went ahead and ended his life.

Although that story may be fictitious, I wonder how many people we pass in a day who would have jumped off that bridge if we were the last person who had the chance to speak to them. There are simple things that you might like to say, such as:

"What a pretty coat!"
"You have such polite children!"
"How beautiful a day to be out today is, isn't it!"
"The Lord Jesus is to be praised."

These kinds of sayings may be rare and they might even seem forced or unnatural. But even simply a smile or an acknowledgment of the other person's presence can do wonders to help an individual in need of encouragement. Uplifting words are addressed to people who are sad, afraid, upset, discouraged, or lonely—and they need to be words that lift people up or that are comforting, protecting, understanding, and encouraging. God Himself, as it is recorded in Hebrews 13:5, says this: "I will never leave you nor forsake you." And that is so comforting.

To encourage is to give courage, hope, or confidence.

Encouraging words are powerful. They can inspire the downcast to reach for new plateaus, because they give hope!

Thankful Words

We are most thankful when we are most humble. And humble, appreciative people are a joy to be with, even just for who they are in themselves. Gratitude is something that spreads cheer to both the giver and the receiver.

Loving Words

All words flow from varying degrees of love, whether love toward my neighbor or acquaintances, or toward family or friends. The same is also true, that unkind words flow from varying degrees of hate. A related point is that our nonverbal demeanor complements our words. And so the following statement makes very good sense:

Your talk talks, and your walk talks,
but your walk talks louder than your talk talks.

A special form of kindness is "kindness on the way." Consider the following:

- Smiles travel miles and bring cheer wherever they go.
- A smile acknowledges the value of someone and conveys a hello to a fellow human being.
- A smile can communicate that you're special.
- A smile can provide a glimmer of hope.

- A smile of encouragement can say, "Hang in there," or, "I understand."

In the Small Things . . .
Sometimes even a wink can convey special thoughts. Small courtesies take very little time or effort, and these are the kinds of things that you could do:

- Open the door for someone, or help an elderly lady.
- Tip generously.
- Pick up an item someone drops.
- Say please and thank you.
- At social gatherings sit with whomever is alone, and then strike up a conversation. All it takes is to be aware of the people around us to sense their needs and help if we can.

> "LORD, USE ME TODAY TO HELP SERVE
>
> SOMEONE AND HONOR YOU."

Someone once prayed these words: "Lord, use me today to help serve someone and honor You." Cheerful words send out ripples of warmth. Some people may think that this is frivolous fluff, but I've seen people's faces lighten up with a little exchange of some kind words.

Acts of kindness and kind words can open the door to the greatest kindness of all, telling someone the good news of the gospel of Jesus.

A Blanket of Kindness

In James 5:16 we read that the effectual fervent prayer of a righteous man avails much. We need to pray for God's blessing on our efforts of kindness. Praying is also a means of showing kindness. Kindness is beautiful, not only in the act of receiving but especially in the act of giving. You practice kindness no matter what happens. Remember at the end of the account of the Good Samaritan how Jesus concluded with these words: "Go and do likewise."

> WE NEED TO PRAY FOR GOD'S BLESSING ON OUR EFFORTS OF KINDNESS.

Power of Encouragement:

Here are four great ways to offer encouragement; see if you can find ways of putting them into effect today:

1. Be focused. One thing that helps to offer encouragement is to maintain focused attention on the individual you are seeking to encourage. Too often, people are busy, and understandably so, as they are trying to do everything they can to bring glory to God. But along the way, there are people who need some attention for themselves if they are to be encouraged.

Jesus faced an incredibly busy schedule. There were meetings, confrontations, and training sessions with His disciples. There were long walks, big decisions, and magnificent healings. The disciples were overwhelmed by what Jesus accomplished. But He always had time for individuals. He always gave them His full attention. Even when dying on the cross for the whole world, the Lord took the time to help one individual find his way into the kingdom of God as that man, a repenting criminal, called on Jesus to remember him.

2. *Be affirmative.* It is so helpful for people to know they are special, unique, and quite unlike any other person God ever created. Solomon reminds us in one of his well-known proverbs that we must study the uniqueness of each child so that we will be able to properly train that little one. Proverbs 22:6 directs us to train up a child in the way he should go and states that when he is old he will not depart from it. The idea is that a child should be trained according to his natural bent. God puts a certain formula in every uniquely created child, and that formula is the challenge for parents to figure out. So that child, whether younger or older, is in ongoing need of individual affirmation. To achieve individual affirmation, we need to spend time studying, looking, listening, and observing so that we can, in turn, encourage with that affirmation tailored in a careful way for each person.

3. *Be appreciative.* People enjoy hearing that they have done a great job! God has created us in such a way that we do love ourselves. As we've already considered in Chapter 2, He tells us that we are to love others in the same way that we love ourselves. He wants us to extend and apply that appreciation that we have for ourselves with the focus on others. To achieve such genuine appreciation is going to mean that we must know that individual very well. It takes effort and determination to sincerely appreciate what someone else does. God tells

us that we are to esteem others better than ourselves (see Philippians 2:3), and that is never seen nearly as much as when one extends genuine appreciation. Extending that recognition means we are saying the other person is better than we are, and unfortunately, people think so highly of themselves that they easily forget about others. You should show genuine appreciation even if it means you are making the point that they are better than you, because in God's sight He wants us to love them in the same way that we love ourselves.

> IT TAKES EFFORT AND DETERMINATION TO SINCERELY APPRECIATE WHAT SOMEONE ELSE DOES.

4. *Be affectionate.* In God's design, He has created us to appreciate touch. Unfortunately, in our day and age, touch can be misconstrued or misunderstood. But to truly be above board and to share physical affection is a wonderful gift. It is quite common in our society for men to shake hands with men, and it's also quite customary in many cases for men to hug men. Giving a hug to a friend or a man in great need is a wonderful encouragement, and no words need to be expressed. At the same time, because of our society, it is quite difficult to express affection appropriately from a man to a woman. Therefore, it is good for women to share that encouragement with other women and for men to be mindful or to be wary of this. Perhaps a smile and a gentle handshake satisfactorily and appropriately express physical affection.

I would say, then, when it comes to physical affection, one thing each of us can give to another is a smile. Heartfelt focused attention with the eyes and a genuine smile of affirmation will go a long way in encouraging other people.

Points for Awareness and Action

- Showing encouragement to others is a highly intentional matter. You have to learn to think beyond yourself to the needs and circumstances of others. You will be amazed by how much people appreciate this!

- This chapter has emphasized four points in particular—attention, affirmation, appreciation, and affection. Map out in your mind how you can strategically cultivate the grace of encouraging others by applying these matters.

8

ENCOURAGEMENT
in
PERSONAL PRIORITIES

Putting First Things First

Let each of us please his neighbor for his good, to build him up.

(Romans 15:2)

Practical Pointers on How to Be a Good Encourager

Here are several thoughts that are intended to direct you in the way you make encouraging others a priority in your own life. You may find that you have to cycle through the lists and ideas several times before you are able to map out the best ways to naturally and instinctively show encouragement.

1. Good encouragers have to be *genuine*! From Romans 12:9 you are told that you cannot be a phony. Let love be without hypocrisy. Don't fake it but be real.

2. Good encouragers are *diligent*. They are hard workers. It takes courage to encourage. As Romans 12:11 says, we are to be not lagging in diligence, but, instead, fervent in spirit, serving the Lord.

3. Good encouragers are *assertive*. They take initiative. As Romans 12:13 says "distributing to the needs of the saints, given to hospitality." The reason why many people are not encouraged is because everybody else thinks that somebody else is doing the encouraging. Take the initiative and encourage.

4 Good encouragers are *selfless*. They are concerned primarily for others. As Romans 12:14-15 teaches, you are to "bless those who persecute you, bless and do not curse. Rejoice with those who rejoice, and weep with those who weep."

5. "Be of the same mind toward one another, do not set your mind on high things but associate with the humble" (Romans 12:16). Often we look to encourage only those people who are at our level. What about the homeless person who walks in and sits down next to us? What about the unlovely person? The shabbily dressed? The one who is socially awkward? One who is arrogant and prideful? The one who is selfish? Encouragement is expected and appreciated and it will probably be amazing to you to find that when you encourage someone, your opinion of that person will change as well.

The Ten Commandments of friendship[2]

1. Speak to people. There is nothing as nice as a cheerful word of greeting.
2. Smile at people. It takes 72 muscles to frown, but only 14 to smile.
3. Call people by their name. The sweetest music to anyone's ear is the sound of their own name.
4. Be friendly and helpful. If you have friends, be friendly.
5. Be cordial. Speak and act as if everything you do were a real pleasure. This means that you might have to ask yourself questions such as: What about the homeless person? What about the unloved or unlovely person? What about someone who is shabbily dressed?

---

[2] Source unknown.

6. Be genuinely interested in people. You can like every-one if you try!
7. Be generous with praise, cautious with criticism. Try for a ratio of seven praises to each criticism.
8. Be considerate of the feelings of others.
9. Be thoughtful of the opinions of others. People love their opinions as they do their own children; calling them ugly won't get you anything but anger.
10. Be alert to give service. What counts most in life is what we do for others!

Barnabas, a Biblical Example of Encouragement

As a landowner in Cyprus, which was a productive fertile island in the eastern Mediterranean, we may assume that Barnabas was a wealthy man. We know for sure that he was one of those rare men who had the view that life consists of helping and encouraging others. In fact, in every place where he shows up in the New Testament record, he is doing just that.

This man was such an incurable motivator that the apostles finally changed his name from Joses so that he became Barnabas, which means "Son of Encouragement" (see Acts 4:36). If he were on the scene today we might call him Mr. Encouragement. Barnabas was not just a backslapping stroker, however; he was a sincere man of God. He is described as a good man full of the Holy Spirit and of faith—see Acts 11:24.

Barnabas was good in the sense that he was generous. He was kind. He wasn't passive about his goodness either; his virtue was active. He proactively involved himself in the lives of others.

It's not overstating things to say that Barnabas was good in the sense that God is good. His goodness came from a special relationship, in that he was filled with the Holy Spirit, the One who controlled him. And Barnabas was filled with faith—faith in God and faithfulness in representing God. That's the kind of man he was: full of the Holy Spirit and full of faith.

There are three transferable qualities from Barnabas' life that can direct us as we encourage others:

1. *A Barnabas says what he means, and means what he says.* The book of the Acts of the Apostles tells us about the first-century believers who sold their possessions and divided them among all as anyone had need. The account records that Ananias and Sapphira claimed that they had sold everything and brought the money to the feet of the apostles—but in fact they had kept back some of the money for their own use. As a result, in their lie, they were struck dead. Barnabas, however, acting in truth and integrity, was seen to be a great example. Barnabas's gift was genuine, sincere, and without hypocrisy.

If we are not careful, we can covet the recognition of being an encourager without fulfilling the requirements that go with the role. It takes complete sacrifice to be a servant and to be an encouragement! If we are not careful we can fall into that same lie of pretending.

2. *A Barnabas sees the best in the other person.* Another example that we see in Barnabas is when Paul (at that time still known as Saul of Tarsus) was converted on the road to Damascus. After this miraculous event, instead of persecuting the followers

of Christ, Paul desired to join them. But they were too afraid of him, and understandably so, given how vicious his opposition had been to the gospel they loved. So Barnabas, who had heard of Paul's testimony, believed in Paul and was willing to stick his neck out for him. Encouragers always see potential when others see problems. When no one wanted to do anything with Paul, Barnabas stood up with him and for him; he believed in him.

> ENCOURAGERS ALWAYS SEE POTENTIAL
> WHEN OTHERS SEE PROBLEMS.

3. *A Barnabas shows more concern for others than for himself.* Acts 11:23 states that when Barnabas came and had seen the grace of God, he was glad and encouraged them all that with one purpose of heart, they should continue with the Lord. Barnabas' encouragement fanned the flames that were already burning brightly, and a great many people were added to the Lord.

So while Barnabas ran the risk of gaining a measure of notoriety, he decided nevertheless to go down to Tarsus to find Paul. He was more interested in the cause of Christ than he was in his own cause.

> *No one cares how much you know*
> *until they know how much you care!*

The Importance of Encouragement

A typical dictionary definition of encouragement is that it is the act of inspiring others with renewed courage, renewed spirit, or renewed hope. In the New Testament the word most often translated as "encouragement" is *paraklesis*. This term comes from two Greek words: *para*, meaning "alongside of" and *kaleo*, meaning "to call." When people come alongside us during difficult times to give us renewed courage, a renewed spirit, renewed hope, that's true encouragement.

AN ENCOURAGER IS ONE WHO PUTS

COURAGE INTO THE FAINTHEARTED.

Again and again we find that the term *paraklesis* is the word used in the rallying call; it is the word used of the speeches of leaders and of soldiers who urge each other on. It is the word used of speech which sent fearful and timorous and hesitant soldiers and sailors courageously in the battle. A *parakletos* is therefore an encourager, one who puts courage into the fainthearted, one who nerves the feeble arm for fight, and one who makes a very ordinary person cope gallantly with the perilous and dangerous situation. The word *parakalein* is the word for exhorting others to noble deeds and high thoughts.

To me, it is especially the word of courage before battle. Life is always calling us into the battle. And this point is a really important one: the One who makes us able to stand up to the opposing forces, to cope with life in a conquering manner, is the *Parakletos*, the Holy Spirit, the third Person of the Trinity.

The Holy Spirit is none other than the presence and power of the risen Christ.

Encouragement, often described and commanded in the New Testament, is an important character ministry for us to develop and practice.

Points for Awareness and Action

- From the various lists in this chapter, identify five areas in which you can plan to follow these guidelines. Be sure to put at least two of these into effect in the next week, and be sure to apply all five of them within the next four weeks.

- Jesus, sometimes referred to as a friend who sticks closer than a brother, is a great encourager. He encourages us especially by His Holy Spirit. Suggest three ways in which you can draw alongside others and become an instrument of love and grace to them in their discouragement.

9

ENCOURAGEMENT
in
FRIENDSHIP

The Care and Nurture of Others

Blessed be the God and Father of our Lord Jesus Christ, the Father of mercies and God of all comfort, who comforts us in all our affliction, so that we may be able to comfort those who are in any affliction, with the comfort with which we ourselves are comforted by God.

(2 Corinthians 1:3-4)

David and Jonathan had a remarkable friendship, wonderfully recorded for us in the Old Testament. It serves as a model for friendships today. We may draw lines of application from their relationship to the circumstances we encounter in our needy days, whether in a family setting or in work and education.

Think of the friendship these two had. Each was willing to do what was best for the other, no matter what loss they would experience.

Jonathan was the heir apparent to be king because Saul had been appointed by God to be king. Therefore, as culture would have it, Jonathan should be the next king. David was brought into the mix simply as a shepherd boy who could play the harp. He was brought in to help calm King Saul's foul moods. There was nothing that spoke of his being even remotely qualified to become king of Israel one day. He wasn't even old enough or strong enough to be a soldier to fight the Philistines. And he wasn't in the right family to be king.

Somewhere along the line as Jonathan and David were becoming friends, Saul began trying to kill David. He was becoming more and more aware that David was to replace him as king. His moods would be such that he would literally try to impale David with his spear. If David's harp-playing didn't get the expected result—King Saul much calmer and relaxed—then David would have to flee for his life.

Not only was Jonathan the heir apparent, but David knew God wanted him, David, to be king. David was aware that he was fighting and fleeing for his life. Saul, a great warrior in his own right, was after David. As David began to sense this more strongly, he and Jonathan met to discuss what they should do about it. David knew that Jonathan would help him know what the king expected of him, and once that was determined, he would either stay or flee.

Their final meeting must have been a very emotional and tough one. They had formed this wonderful friendship, but they knew that it wasn't going to work for David to remain. Jonathan's father was intent on killing him, and that wasn't what either of the young men wanted. David knew that Jonathan had his best interest at heart, and Jonathan knew that David was feeling the same toward him. They parted, and their fears were realized, as they never saw each other again this side of heaven.

> DAVID KNEW THAT JONATHAN HAD HIS BEST INTEREST AT HEART, AND JONATHAN KNEW THAT DAVID WAS FEELING THE SAME TOWARD HIM.

However, their example is critically important in the area of encouragement, as each sought the best for his friend no matter what either of their own personal aspirations may have been. Esteeming others better than oneself, as Christ commanded, helps friends overlook their own comforts, and seek to extend helpfulness to the other, no matter what it costs. Encouraging one another helps friendships blossom and grow, as well as help to lift up one who may be burdened under the cares of this world.

The Old Man

The story is told of an employer who began to make fun and who often spoke in derogatory terms about one of his employees. The man always came to work in old clothes and always brought his lunch in a brown paper bag. He would always fold that brown paper bag back up after lunch and would use it again the next day for transporting his lunch. He was not a well-versed man, and neither did he have a lot of friends, but he was always loyal and faithful to his job.

One day, the employer decided to follow him home and, from a distance, try to find out why this man was so loyal and faithful to his work and yet wore such old clothes and revealed how poor he was by using the same lunch bag over and over again. When the employer got within a certain distance of the man's home, he saw exactly where it was that he lived. He walked up to the door knocked on it. When he was invited in, he found the reason for this man's lack of expensive clothing and he discovered why he was so tight with his money. He was caring for his invalid wife and was pouring all of his money into her care. That changed the employer's perspective of why this man looked and acted in the ways he did.

The Bowling Alley

Another story very vivid in my mind involves a man who was bowling in a bowling alley. It was years ago. This was at the time when the pins were put back into the receiver by hand, and nothing was automated. So this man was bowling and the person at the other end seemed to be dawdling and taking his time when he was putting the pins back in order. The bowler began to be impatient and holler down the alley for the unseen man back there to speed up his work. He did this repeatedly and finally, in his impatience, he went and reported the incident to the manager of the bowling alley. Within minutes he saw, much to his shame and embarrassment, what he had just done: the man who was "taking his time" was actually a man with one leg much shorter than the other. There was no doubt he was doing all he could to keep up with moving the bowling pins but because of his physical malady he just could not do that as speedily as others might have. The visitor to the alley had spoken harshly and hurt a man's livelihood just because of his own selfishness and because he had not tried to gain the perspective of the other individual.

For us to share words that are fitly spoken—for us to be an encouragement to others—we need to see life as best we can from their perspective and not think ours is the only pattern! And, what better way to see life from another person's perspective than from Christ's? If you are going to encourage as you ought, you are going to not only note that you should, but also have a right reason to continue. As Jesus once said, the spirit is willing, but the flesh is weak!

Some Questions to Think About

- Parents how do you speak to your children, regardless of your age or theirs?
- Parents, how do you speak to your married children?
- How do you speak to your children that are in your home?
- And those that are your in-laws, how do you speak to them?

- Children, how do you speak to your parents? Are you bitter about what you don't have or when you think of what you *do* have?
- Friends, do you try to encourage your friends and uplift them or simply direct them?
- Spouses, are you building up and edifying your husband or wife?
- Grandparents, do you recognize all your grandchildren have to offer?
- Employer, are you a spoken encouragement to your employees?
- Employees, are you appreciative of your job?

Points for Awareness and Action

- Consider the example of the employer who found out about his employee and his dedication to the care and nurture of his invalid wife. Do you know of other stories such as this one? In your own words, express the primary lesson to be learned from such incidents.

- How would you best develop a strategy to find out about a negative situation before judging what appears to be the cause?

10

ENCOURAGEMENT
in
CONSECRATION

Living Life Wholly for God

I appeal to you therefore, brothers, by the mercies of God, to present your bodies as a living sacrifice, holy and acceptable to God, which is your spiritual worship.

(Romans 12:1)

Consecration is a word that is not used today as much as it has been in days gone past. In this context, it has the idea of being dedicated completely and consistently for God and for his use. The hymn writer could express it this way:

> *Take my life, and let it be*
> *Consecrated, Lord, to thee*

James, in the letter that bears his name, was insistent on this point: it is as we draw near to God that He will draw near to us. See James 4: 6-8 and consider especially the promise of the last sentence:

> Therefore it says, "God opposes the proud but gives grace to the humble." Submit yourselves therefore to God. Resist the devil, and he will flee from you. Draw near to God, and he will draw near to you.

The last part of the quote above is a wonderful promise that, as we draw near to God—in the reading of his Word, in prayer, in meeting with his people, in living intentionally as holy and useful a life as possible—He, the Infinite Creator and Redeemer, will meet with us in a warm and personal relationship.

You will find that there is a correlation between your relationship with God and your relationship with people. Just as in the vertical and horizontal structure of the cross of Calvary, our lives are designed to function in both realms. Only as you are in a redeemed relationship with God—through repentance toward God and saving faith in his Son the Lord Jesus Christ— will you be able truly to be an encourager to other people.

The Bible makes it very clear in 1 John 4:9-11 that

> In this the love of God was made manifest among us, that God sent his only Son into the world, so that we might live through him. In this is love, not that we have loved God but that he loved us and sent his Son to be the propitiation for our sins. Beloved, if God so loved us, we also ought to love one another.

When we live a life of redeemed and reconciled usefulness to God, we will find that we begin to model the grace that He first showed to us.

Points for Awareness and Action

- Think about how the Lord Jesus came down from heaven to be born, live, die, and rise again for ordinary people like you and me. We didn't love Him—in fact, we were unlovely; and yet He showed his love to us and while we were yet sinners, Christ died for us (Romans 5:8).

- "To be an encouragement to others, I will intentionally live a life of consecration to God." Discuss this quotation and how it might apply to you in light of your practical circumstances in day-to-day life.

Appendix 1

Quotable Quotes to Think About

- The six most important words are: "I admit I made a mistake."
- The five most important words are: "You did a good job."
- The four most important words you use are: "What is your opinion?"
- The three most important words to use are: "If you please."
- The two most important words to use are: "Thank you."
- The most important word to use is the word "We."
- The least important word ever to use is the word "I."

"Speech is the mirror of the soul; as a man speaks, so he is." This was written by a man called Lilia's service Publilius Syrus, in 50 BC. That same man said, "Conversation is the image of the mind. As the man is, so is his talk."

"Speak not but what may benefit others or yourself; avoid trifling conversation." (Ben Franklin, 1798)

"A man is seldom better than his conversation." (German proverb)

"Out of the abundance of the heart the mouth speaks." (Matthew 12:34b)

"Good words are worth much and cost little!" (George Herbert)

"An athlete may be made insufferable by praise. Once a day, a truly deserving athlete may fall by the wayside for the want of it." (A professional coach; he made a point of saying this once a year.)

Appendix 2

Bible Texts to Think About

Romans 1:8-12

First, I thank my God through Jesus Christ for all of you, because your faith is proclaimed in all the world. For God is my witness, whom I serve with my spirit in the gospel of his Son, that without ceasing I mention you always in my prayers, asking that somehow by God's will I may now at last succeed in coming to you. For I long to see you, that I may impart to you some spiritual gift to strengthen you—that is, that we may be mutually encouraged by each other's faith, both yours and mine.

1 Corinthians 1:4-9

I give thanks to my God always for you because of the grace of God that was given you in Christ Jesus, that in every way you were enriched in him in all speech and all knowledge—even as the testimony about Christ was confirmed among you—so that you are not lacking in any gift, as you wait for the revealing of our Lord Jesus Christ, who will sustain you to the end, guiltless in the day of our Lord Jesus Christ. God is faithful, by whom you were called into the fellowship of his Son, Jesus Christ our Lord.

Colossians 4:6

Let your speech always be gracious, seasoned with salt, so that you may know how you ought to answer each person.

Psalm 19:14

Let the words of my mouth and the meditation of my heart be acceptable in your sight, O Lord, my rock and my redeemer.

John 13:35

. . . by this shall all men know that you are my disciples, if you have love for one another.

Applying Some Other Bible Texts

Hebrews 10:22 helps us consider and give attention to continuous care, watching over one another, studying how we may stir and stimulate insight to love and helpful deeds and noble activities. In Hebrews 10:25 God actually encourages us in His Word to meet together.

In 1 Thessalonians 2:11, 14 we are told to encourage each other and edify each other just as [we] are doing. The brethren were actually exhorted to warn those who are unruly, encourage the fainthearted, and uphold the weak and be patient with all.

Churches today are made up of memberships, and whether small in size or in the thousands, the pastor of the church and the church staff are in no way going to be able encourage every single individual on a personal and individual basis. Therefore it is vitally important that every member of a church become an encourager.

Books that Helped Me

I am indebted to many writers and speakers for the contents of this book and in particular I owe a debt of gratitude to the following for their help in various chapters as detailed below:

Chapter 1: *The Psychology of Encouragement*, Magazine article in the Counseling Psychologist, FO Main and SR Boughner, New York, NY, 2011.

Chapter 2: Chapter 4, Chapter 5: *So You Want to Be Like Christ, Eight Essentials to get you there,* W. Publishing Group, Nashville, TN, 2005

Chapter 6: *The Jesus Creed, Loving God, Loving Others*, Paraclete Press, Brewster, Massachusetts, 2004

Chapter 7, Chapter 8: *The Power of Encouragement*, David Jeremiah, Multnomah Publishers, Orange, CA 1997
The Power of Encouragement, Calvin Miller, Tyndale House Publishers, Inc. Wheaton, Illinois, 2003

Resources

- *1,000 Mitzvahs...How small acts of kindness can heal, inspire, and change your life.* Linda Cohen, Seal Press, Berkeley, CA, 1968
- *Powerful Practices of Really Great Mentors, How to inspire and motivate anyone,* Stephen E. Kohn and Vincent D. O'Connell, Prince Frederick, MD, 2015
- *Your Reactions are showing,* J. Allan Petersen, Good News Broadcasting Association, United States, 1967
- *The Power of Encouragement,* Calvin Miller, Tyndale House Publishers, Inc., Wheaton, Illinois, 2003
- *The Power of Encouragement,* David Jeremiah, Multnomah Publishers, Orange, CA, 1997
- *The Law of Kindness, Serving with heart and hands,* Reformation Heritage Books, Grand Rapids, MI, 2007
- *The Goal of Brotherly Love,* Sword and Trowel, Metropolitan Tabernacle, Elephant and Castle, London, England, 1994
- *The Jesus Creed, Loving God, Loving Others,* Paraclete Press, Brewster, Massachusetts, 2004
- *Joy in the New Testament,* William B. Eerdmans Publishing Company, Paternoster Press, England, 1984
- *So You want to be like Christ. Eight Essentials to get you there,* W. Publishing Group, Nashville, TN, 2005

Connect with John Lehman

https://www.facebook.com/john.lehman.165

Let us encourage one another—I'd just love to hear from you!

Visit my website: www.wordsfitlyspoken.info

John Lehman
www.wordsfitlyspoken.info

It's Apparent . . . You're A Parent

It's Apparent . . . You're a Parent!
Raising Godly Children in Today's World
Durable Hardback, 7 ¼ x 5 inches, 128pp
ISBN: 978-0-9899-532-0-7

I'm a parent. . . Wow! How should I best navigate through the wonderful, new challenges and opportunities that are coming my way? What wisdom may be gleaned from the Bible, God's living Word? Will God really enable the process to turn out well? In six helpful, easy-to-read chapters, John Lehman, a family pastor and himself a parent and grandparent of several children, writes with passion and clarity on the great issues of bringing up children. Here you may read about topics such as

- Getting ready to become a mom or dad
- Preparing an overarching goal for your child
- Demonstrating what it means to live in submission to the one, true God
- Facing the consequences God has directed when there is disobedience
- Cultivating a godly parental model that emphasizes practical godliness
- Navigating wisely through the ages and stages that lead to adulthood

Rich in biblical content, this book will help steer you carefully through the many situations that come the way of all parents.

I Do or I Don't

I Do or I don't
Cultivating a Godly Marriage in Today's World
Durable Hardback, 7 ¼ x 5 inches, 144pp
ISBN: 978-0-9899532-5-2

In any marriage, it is extremely important to recognize that there are certain areas which must be guided and guarded. The five areas which can attract significant challenges and difficulties are as follows: role relationships, communication, physical relationships, finances, and parenting. Throughout this book, biblical content is sought to help couples be all they can be for God's glory, and in so doing, be able to show the world Christ and the Church through their own personal marriage relationship,

Struggling couples should take heart and take notes!
Brad Stille, Pastor of First Baptist Church of Wixom, MI
Gospel truth and biblical principles—this book will take both and bring them to bear on marriage. The Scripture is full of truth that will guide and direct our marriages. So, whether you are soon to be married or have been for years—read, meditate on, and apply the truths in this book.
Jeremy McMorris, Lead Pastor, Liberty Baptist Church, Dalhart, TX
. . . a refreshing resource for couples who desire a Christ-centered, Spirit-empowered marriage.
Ben Ice, Family Life Ministries, Calvary Baptist Church, Simpsonville, SC

Fit for the Master

Fit for the Master
Glorifying God in a Healthy Body
Durable Hardback, 7.8 x 5 inches, Illustrated, 144pp
ISBN: 978-0-9899-532-9-0

Fearfully and wonderfully made—that's how God created you. He crafted you, and you were designed to glorify Him. So, it's important for you to be fit if you are to enjoy life to the fullest!
For this, your body needs the benefits of proper exercise and nutrition. Exercising:

- releases endorphins, helping you feel better;
- enables you to function longer;
- works in tandem with good nutrition;
- enables you to rest well after you have exerted yourself.

In *Fit for the Master*, John Lehman shares valuable insights to help you in developing and maintaining your body—the temple of the Holy Spirit.

www.ingramcontent.com/pod-product-compliance
Lightning Source LLC
Chambersburg PA
CBHW070910160726
48004CB00003B/1314